Distinctions in Nature

Fruits and
Vegetables Explained

Alicia Z. Klepeis

Cavendish
Square

New York

Published in 2017 by Cavendish Square Publishing, LLC
243 5th Avenue, Suite 136, New York, NY 10016

Library of Congress Cataloging-in-Publication Data

Names: Klepeis, Alicia, 1971- author.
Title: Fruits and vegetables explained / Alicia Z. Klepeis.
Description: New York : Cavendish Square Publishing, [2017] |
Series: Distinctions in nature | Includes bibliographical references and index.
Identifiers: LCCN 2016006888 (print) | LCCN 2016009122 (ebook) |
ISBN 9781502620132 (pbk.) | ISBN 9781502617446 (library bound) |
ISBN 9781502617583 (6 pack) | ISBN 9781502617507 (ebook)
Subjects: LCSH: Fruit–Juvenile literature. | Vegetables–Juvenile literature. | Botany–Juvenile literature.
Classification: LCC SB357.2 .K54 2017 (print) | LCC SB357.2 (ebook) |
DDC 575.6/7–dc23
LC record available at http://lccn.loc.gov/2016006888

Editorial Director: David McNamara
Editor: Kelly Spence
Copy Editor: Nathan Heidelberger
Art Director: Jeffrey Talbot
Designer: Stephanie Flecha
Production Assistant: Karol Szymczuk
Photo Research: J8 Media

Printed in the United States of America

Contents

Many colorful fruits and vegetables, such as kiwis and chili peppers, are available for sale at a farmers' market.

Introduction: Eating a Rainbow

S tep into the grocery store. Walk down the **produce** aisle. Do you see fruits and vegetables? Fruits and vegetables are plants. They grow outdoors on every **continent** except Antarctica. There, people grow them in greenhouses. All fruits and vegetables share some things in common. They need water, sunlight, and good soil to grow.

Babies often eat **pureed** fruits or vegetables. Some people enjoy a vegetable salad for dinner. Others choose a fruit salad

A monkey eats a sweet, ripe mango in a tropical forest.

for dessert. Animals also eat fruits and vegetables. Deer in the woods might eat wild mushrooms. Monkeys in the rain forest chomp on bananas or mangoes. Fruits and vegetables provide **nutrients** for living things. They contain vitamins and minerals that help us grow.

Grouping Fruits and Veggies

All fruits and vegetables share some characteristics. But they can also be different from one another in many ways. Some grow in hot places. Others grow where

The leafy tops of carrots, onions, and beets stick out from the soil as they grow.

the weather is cooler. Many fruits, like oranges, grow on trees. Vegetables like onions and carrots grow underground. Fruits are often sweeter than vegetables.

There are thousands of different kinds of fruits and vegetables. Scientists **classify**, or place, them into groups, based on their shared features. **Taxonomy** is the process of classifying living things.

Many tropical fruits grow in Thailand, including mangoes, jackfruits, pineapples, lychees, and dragon fruits.

1 Looking at Fruits and Veggies

People around the world eat fruits like peaches, berries, and limes. Fruits come in different colors, shapes, and sizes. Blueberries are tiny. **Jackfruits** are huge. A single jackfruit can weigh 100 pounds (45 kilograms)!

What Is a Fruit?

So what is a fruit, really? **Botanists** describe a fruit as the part of a flowering plant that develops from its **ovary**. The fruit contains the seeds, protecting them inside.

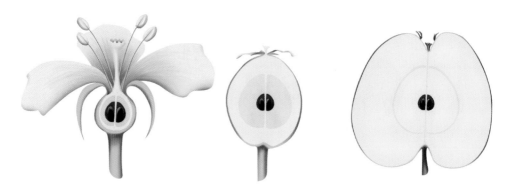

This diagram shows the stages of the life cycle of an apple from flower to fruit. Over time, the apple loses its pink blossoms, and the remaining ovary develops into a fruit that protects the seeds inside.

Spreading Seeds

Fruits are often colorful, sweet, and fleshy. These qualities make fruit a tasty snack for many animals. After an animal eats a fruit, the undigested seeds get passed. This helps to spread the seeds. Before long, new plants will sprout from these seeds. Seeds can also travel on the wind or in the water.

It's Not a Vegetable!

It may seem strange, but many foods we think of as vegetables are actually fruits. Avocados are fruits.

Zoom In

The outside of fruits can be smooth, bumpy, spiky, or even hairy.

Different parts of the celery plant are edible. It is most common to eat the crunchy stalk. However, the tasty leaves and bumpy root are also used in many dishes.

So are tomatoes, squashes, and eggplants. All these fruits share an important quality: they have seeds.

Parts of a Plant That Are Vegetables

Vegetables are basically all the **edible** parts of a plant other than its fruit. These include its leaves, stem, roots, and even flower buds. Spinach and lettuce are the leaves of a plant. Broccoli and cauliflower are flower buds. Celery stalks are actually the stem of a plant. Beets and carrots are roots. A potato is a **tuber**.

Strawberry plants grow above the ground, but their roots lie beneath the soil.

2 A Closer Look

Fruits and vegetables are different in many ways. Let's learn more!

From the Earth

Root vegetables, which are the roots of plants, grow below the ground. These include turnips, carrots, sweet potatoes, and radishes. While the roots of some fruits grow underground, too, the fruit itself grows above the surface of the soil.

You may have seen an apple tree full of ripe fruit in the fall. Cherries, peaches, and

A field of broccoli grows in California. These plants need space between them to grow properly.

oranges also grow on trees. While many fruits grow on trees, vegetables do not. Vegetables normally come from **herbaceous** plants. The stems of herbaceous plants are softer than the woody stems of trees and bushes.

Some fruits, like blueberries, grow on bushes. Others, like pumpkins and squashes, grow on vines. Many vegetables grow above the ground. Some, like broccoli and cabbage, need lots of space.

Kinds of Fruits

It is amazing how many different kinds of fruits and veggies exist. The two main types of fruit are fleshy and dry fruits. In a fleshy fruit, the part of the fruit surrounding its seeds is soft and juicy. Dry fruits include beans and nuts, like almonds. These aren't nearly as juicy as fleshy fruits. Some fruits, like berries and lemons, have many

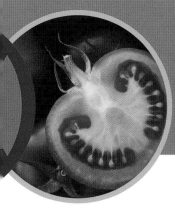

Zoom In

In a fleshy fruit, the section around the seeds is pulpy or juicy.

seeds. Others, like cherries or apricots, only have one seed. It is called a pit.

How Vegetables Grow

You might wonder how vegetables grow if they don't contain seeds inside. Take a carrot, for example. The orange part of the carrot does not contain seeds. But the greens at

Almonds, peanuts, mung beans, and kidney beans are all examples of dry fruits.

These tasty carrots are growing on a farm in Japan. The seeds are found in the greens at the top of the plant.

the top of the carrot do produce seeds. These seeds can be planted to grow new carrots.

Different Veggies

There are many kinds of vegetables in the world. They can be stems, like asparagus or **kohlrabi**. They can be flowers, like broccoli and artichokes. Other vegetables, like cabbage and spinach, are leaves. Onions and

Both garlic and onions are the bulbs of plants. This bulb of garlic is starting to sprout, or put forth new shoots.

garlic are plant **bulbs**, or underground buds of a plant. People eat roots like parsnips and beets as vegetables. A potato is a tasty tuber (underground stem).

Nutritious and Delicious

Both fruits and vegetables are healthy foods. They both have water and **fiber** in them. Many have Vitamins C and A. But fruits and vegetables have some nutritional differences.

Beets are sweet-tasting root vegetables. People often add their leafy tops to soups and salads.

Fruits tend to be higher in **calories** than vegetables. An exception to this rule are denser, starchier vegetables like potatoes or beets.

Green leafy vegetables and broccoli contain **calcium**, which is good for your bones. Most fruits don't contain calcium. But figs and oranges do. Vegetables often contain more protein than fruits. They also are much more likely to contain Vitamin K.

So the next time someone suggests you eat your fruits and veggies, just say yes!

In the Kitchen

People around the world eat fruits and vegetables. Kids might grab an apple or a banana for an after-school

Freshly squeezed juices are a tasty way to enjoy the nutritional benefits of fruits.

People often eat vegetables alongside meat dishes. Broccoli, potatoes, peas, and carrots are served with this roast lamb and gravy.

snack. But it's unlikely that they'd munch on an onion or some kale. Perhaps the difference is in the sweetness. Fruits are generally sweet. They are popular raw, in juice, or as desserts.

Vegetables are usually thought of as **savory**. Most people think of vegetables as something to cook and serve alongside a main dish. You can picture a piece of meat next to some spinach or sweet potatoes. They are often part of soups and stews, too.

1. Kiwis contain hundreds of nutritious, tiny black seeds.

2. The edible skin of a sweet potato is high in fiber.

3 · Be a Food Detective

Be a food detective. Use your knowledge to figure out which of these plants (*left*) are fruits and which are vegetables.

1. This food has furry brown skin. Its flesh is bright green and contains many tiny black seeds. This plant was introduced to the West from East Asia and Japan. Is this plant a fruit or vegetable? Why?

2. This food grows underground. It often has orange flesh under its skin. It does not contain seeds. There are hundreds of varieties of this food grown around the world. Is this plant a fruit or vegetable?

3. Bumpy-skinned avocadoes hang from a tree as they grow. An avocado tree can grow up to 80 feet (24 meters) high.

4. Cabbages come in all sizes and usually weigh between 2 and 7 pounds (0.9 to 3.2 kg).

3. This food grows on a tree. It can have smooth or bumpy skin. Inside, it has creamy green flesh and one giant seed. Is this plant a fruit or vegetable? What qualities give this away?

4. This food grows close to the ground. It comes in different colors like green and purple. People eat its leaves in stir-fries, salads, or even as coleslaw. Is it a fruit or vegetable? Why?

Answer Key:

1. This is a kiwi. It is a fruit because it has seeds.
2. This is a sweet potato. It is a vegetable because its flesh does not contain seeds.
3. This is an avocado. It is a fruit because it contains a seed. Also, only fruits grow on trees.
4. This is a cabbage. It is a vegetable because it is the leaves of a plant.

This sweet watermelon is not naturally seedless. It has been modified to grow that way.

4 Rule Breakers

After reading this far, you know that all fruits contain seeds. But some fruits appear to be rule breakers. You may have eaten seedless grapes. Or maybe even a **clementine** without seeds. Seedless watermelon has grown quite popular in recent years. (Everyone knows they do have traces of seeds, but we can eat those little white ones.)

Some fruits are seedless. This is because scientists have tinkered with them. But these plants still count as fruits. In short, if a plant naturally has seeds but has been **genetically modified** to not have them, it is still a fruit.

Bananas and Berries

Bananas are one of the most popular fruits around the world. But did you know that a banana plant is actually an herb? People talk about banana "trees," but banana

Bananas are green while growing but turn yellow as they ripen.

Fruits and Vegetables Explained

Grapes, red currants, red gooseberries, and persimmons are all true berries. They are fleshy inside.

plants are actually herbaceous plants. Their stems do not contain woody tissue like real trees do.

Many people are surprised to find out that the part of the banana plant we eat is actually a berry. A true berry stems from one flower with one ovary. A berry normally has several seeds. Bananas, tomatoes, pomegranates, and kiwis are all true berries.

The next time you go to the grocery store, look at all the colorful fruits and vegetables. Can you tell which is which?

botanists Scientists who study plants.

bulbs Underground plant structures that contain buds protected by papery skin.

calcium A soft, whitish-gray element that is found in the bodies of most plants and animals.

calories Units used to measure the energy in foods.

classify To group based on similarities.

clementine A tangerine of a deep orange-red color that is grown around the Mediterranean and in South Africa.

continent One of the great divisions of land on Earth, such as North America or Asia.

edible Safe or fit to be eaten.

fiber Mostly indigestible material in food that stimulates the intestines during digestion.

genetically modified To have changed how a fruit or vegetable grows to produce a more desirable characteristic.

herbaceous Referring to a stem with little or no woody tissue.

jackfruits The very large edible fruits of the fast-growing jackfruit tree, found in Asia.

kohlrabi A type of cabbage with a swollen, turnip-like stem that is edible.

nutrients Substances that provide nourishment needed for growth and the maintenance of life.

ovary The enlarged, rounded, lower part of the pistil of a flower where the seeds are formed.

produce Fresh fruits and vegetables, such as those grown on a farm.

pureed Boiled then run through a sieve or blender until smooth and soft, as in fruits and vegetables.

savory Something that is salty or spicy rather than sweet.

taxonomy The orderly classification of plants and animals according to their natural relationships.

tuber The thickened underground part of a stem (or rhizome) that bears buds from which new plants grow.

Find Out More

Books

Agarwal, Tanya Luther. *Fruits and Vegetables.* Weird and Wonderful. New Delhi, India: The Energy and Resources Institute, 2011.

Gibbons, Gail. *The Fruits We Eat.* New York: Holiday House, 2016.

Woolf, Alex. *You Wouldn't Want To Live Without Vegetables!* You Wouldn't Want to Live Without. New York: Scholastic, 2016.

Websites

Difference Between Fruits and Vegetables
www.youtube.com/watch?v=HqjXqvr_l1o
Watch this video for a simple explanation of the difference between fruits and vegetables.

Fresh for Kids
www.freshforkids.com.au/index.html
Learn all about different fruits and veggies.

Index

Page numbers in **boldface** are illustrations.

About the Author

Alicia Klepeis loves to research fun and out-of-the-ordinary topics that make nonfiction exciting for readers. Klepeis began her career at the National Geographic Society. She is the author of many kids' books, including *The World's Strangest Foods*, *Bizarre Things We've Called Medicine*, *Francisco's Kites*, and *From Pizza to Pisa*. She lives with her family in upstate New York.